FORTUNA

Gawain Douglas

Fortuna

LORD GAWAIN DOUGLAS

HERLA

Published by
HERLA PUBLISHING, an imprint of

ALMA BOOKS LTD
London House
243–253 Lower Mortlake Road
Richmond
Surrey TW9 2LL
United Kingdom
www.almabooks.com

Fortuna first published by Herla, an imprint of Alma Books Ltd, in 2009
Copyright © Lord Gawain Douglas, 2009

Lord Gawain Douglas asserts his moral right to be identified as the author of
this work in accordance with the Copyright, Designs and Patents Act 1988
Printed in Great Britain by TJ International, Padstow, Cornwall

ISBN: 978-1-84688-088-9

For Nicolette

Contents

The Place of Poetry

I live in a big white town house, in an Edwardian square by the sea in Kent. It has pleasant gardens with tennis courts and croquet lawns and a nice clubhouse. I often go there and play tennis in the summer, and every day winter and summer I go to the pebbled shore and gaze across the waters. Mostly they are grey and dull and one could be anywhere; sometimes they are blue and sunstruck and then I'm in the best place in the world. I have a kind wife, and children who've all left home, and I go to work every day and come back late and eat and drink rather a lot. And that's my life really.

But oh! I nearly forgot: at the top of my house there's a further floor, a sort of attic which is always locked and which has a hidden key. Most of the time this key is very difficult to find. Sometimes I even forget it exists. Then one day, puzzled, walking up the stairs perhaps, or in a brown study, looking out into the rain, I'll see it shining somewhere, beckoning me. Then I'll pick it up quite naturally as though it's been there all the time, and climb the stairs and unlock the door to that other place; the place where poetry is.

I cannot tell you any more about it or what it means, or how it came about. Your guess is quite as good as mine.

On the Beach

Six Moments, Osea Island, Essex

1

The winter sun touches the chair.
My guest speaks on
But my thoughts
Are poised
On the edge of the unknown.

2

The wind today
Blowing troubles
Away.

A giant hand
Empties
My mind.

3

He touched my arm
An old friend
From the past
To warm my heart
Unfold my faculties
Like marvellous flowers
That slept.

Dear old sun
Every spring you
Remind me
Every winter
I forget.

4

Alfred A longed to be free
As he made love.

Bucking and tossing
He heard the rain
Against
The window.
He thought
"One day I shall ride in
From the North Sea
Utterly alone
On the back of the wind.
My wild cry
Will pierce the night
And disturb the embrace
Of dejected lovers."

5

The moon is after me tonight
He caught sight of me
Just now
And marked me
For a moonman.
I feel him everywhere,
Behind my back
Above my head.
Soon I must go
To our bay window
And have it out
With him.
My blood will be
Liquid silver,
My heart a
Silver stone
And my soul
A moonbeam.

6

Jabber jabber goes the moon
To me,

Her words dance the water
To my heart.
Quick, quick they run and leap
To me
Who turns chilled, away from
Such black art.

The Blackwater Estuary, 1.00 a.m.

On a Street Corner

Don't go down to the shops just now,
There is infinite chance, just here,
On this square of pavement.
Look how the wind has tossed your hair
And quickened your wit,
The sun warmed your blood.
See the rush-hour people as they pass,
Even they are touched by spring
And smile, as if almost remembering.
Look! Just before leaving, the day
Has thrown her loveliest colours
Across the street.
Don't go, don't go,
Now can last for ever if you stay.

Blackheath, London, one evening in May 1972

Window Dresser

Lady in the shop window with
Your hips indefinitely poised
I join your infinite (sartorial)
Contemplation.
In this rush-hour river
You are an imperturbable lily,
In this desert, a green palm
Which gives a moment's shade.

King's Road, London, 22nd November 1974

Explain Yourself

If you ask me what I mean
I cannot say.
I only know
At odd moments of
Strange encounter
With myself
And sunlight
Sometimes,
Looking down a
Canterbury street
As though it were
A telescope
Fixed on eternity.
Then,
I could tell you,
Maybe,
If you didn't ask me,
What I mean.

6th May 1978

Dover Harbour

Who could have thought
One could be free
In Dover Harbour?
A strange place,
Full of blocks of flats
And "pay and display" signs.
However, the beach in front
And certain faded gleams
Of sunlight on blue water
Led me back.
A boy again
On Cornish sands
I played the length of
Lazy summer days and
Lived a brilliant shining dream
Without beginning, and
No fall of night to come.

13th July 1990

Daffodils

I had to turn my face away
Seeing you just now.
February is too early,
You should have been asleep still,
The ground hard
Denying you access
To the light.

All sorts of things were unready,
The days too short,
The light grey,
My spirits too fragile by far
For such an encounter.

I should have been protected really
Winter should have wrapped
Her kind coat around my shoulders
And sent me packing home.

So I had to turn my face away
Seeing you just now,
Not answering your smile at all.
Smiles can hurt you know,
Colours can cut.
And yellow is a difficult colour.

February 1993

Nicolette

There is a garden in my mind
And you will always be
There round some corner, where I'll find
You by a flower or tree,
And waiting just for me.

The years must take their cruel toll
For idle time we spend,
But you will stay my prettiest girl
Always, and to the end
By far my greatest friend.

13th March 1993

A Mother Comes and Goes

When you first came to stay
There was cherry blossom
On the road beneath
Your window.

You remarked on its beauty then
And in later years
This provided solace
Among frequent sorrows.

Now, they have cut
The inconvenient branches
And you are gone
From your window also.

There is no fall of pink
On the road
This spring.

24th March 1993

Lines Inspired by the Fowey River, Bodmin Moor

I hope I know still
Where the river flows
In that space
Of Cornwall.

A man and a river
Are a fine thing,
I have discovered.

Striding out together
In any weather
Winking and smiling
As they pass,
Making rude remarks.

Their faces shining
Each in the other,
They bring out the best
In one another.

I certainly don't want
Any later heaven
Or pleasure even
Here and now.

Just me and the river
The river my brother.
Just the two of us
Striding out together.

March 1993

An Italian's Funeral in the Isle of Man

In the cold church
On the northern isle
An Italian man
Was prayed to rest.

Few friends were there
To say the words
For him, but those
He loved the best,
Street kids –
He had been one in Italy –
Had come to say goodbye.

In the cold church
On the northern isle
I read the prayer
For the Italian man.

My words were transparent water
From the island hills.
I had not seen words
So clear before.

No sign or message came
From sea-green skies,
Darker, less generous than Italy's
Above the church.

But something shone
Not in stained glass
Or candlelight,
But bright in the
Children's eyes.

It was a light, yes
And a love too,
Something southern
He had brought with him
And never lost,
Had freely given
To the children.
Something that does live on.

13th April 1993

Love's Long Since Cancelled Woe

When you, Madam, went away
The summer quickly took itself southward.
I watched it go despairingly
And thought it was for ever.

The seasons turned upon their wheel
The sorrows upon their circle also.
I watched them both.

The sun sank into a far corner of the sky
Taking my heart with it.

Storms shook the attic window
Frosts scratched at your window pane.
Where were you then?

Now summer has returned,
Early sunlight touches
The empty coverlet.
Dust settles on your bed.

Are you the sunlight
Streaming through the dust?
Are you the blackbird's song,
So beautiful below?

May 1993

Visitors at Supper Time

It was an evening in June.
The white roses peeped
Around the corner
Of the garden.
There was a group of them.

They stood there arm in arm
Smiling into the room,
Nosy things, like
Schoolgirls waiting
To be noticed.

I noticed them all right
And smiled back
Through the open door
While I ate my supper.
I rather fancied them.

They often come out
For a stroll and a chat
With their white dresses on,
And look in at me
On June evenings now.

Solstice at 45

The turning light,
The turning light.
At 2.45 a.m.
The changing light.

The mind as well
Can turn
May turn
Can change
May change
Have light
Have light
At 45
And 2.45.

So strange a light,
A changing light,
But will there ring
No church bell right out,
In this silence
Of midsummer night,
When in the sky
And in my mind
There is a turning light
A changing light?

21st June 1993

A Portrait

This sunlight has been here before,
At this instant exactly
On some similar evening
In July, long ago probably,
But on this pale patch of wall
Over the fireplace.

It has shone here before
Previous to my occupation
Of this space and time
And will again shine afterwards.

Now, it illuminates
My father's portrait,
Inflames his hands
From oil to blood.

Briefly they live, extend,
Hold out to me
Something I had lost,
Forgotten, or never known
Perhaps.

I raise my hand and smile.
Will sunlight alchemize
The past and present
Into love?

The thought is like a switch
For now it fades.
The setting sun is responsible
For innumerable visions,
And this was one.

My father's fingers resume their
Stonelike incommunicableness,
Their enigmatic death.
That which was offered
Is now withdrawn

And I am but a ghost,
A shadow, that has
No explanation.

Lines to My Father

Father, Father
Far away from me,
Will I see you
Will I, will I,
Will we meet then
You and I,
Meet in the unending sea?

Father, Father,
So far apart from me,
Further than the eye can see
Further than the mind can be,
So far, so far.

But Father, Father,
Come we closer
You and I now,
Closer as I end the journey,
Closer as the river widens,
As it nears the endless sea?

And will my spirit know you Father,
Oh will it, will it,
So your son can touch you Father,
Touch your spirit with my spirit,
When we merge together Father,
Merge in the unending sea?

12th September 1996

Twelve Three

The time is three minutes past twelve
And I am twelve stone and three pounds
Exactly.

My height is five feet and nine inches,
And my chest forty-four inches,
Precisely.

The time is now four minutes past twelve
And I am still twelve stone and three pounds,
Exactly.

It is only by repeating these things
That one can understand them,
Correctly.

There is an ache in my heart,
But if I sit totally still it will pass,
Directly.

The time is now five minutes past twelve
And I remain twelve stone and three pounds,
Exactly.

In Praise of the Skull

The skull will out
And so the teeth,
Forget the flesh
Don't scan the face
But seek the skull
That's underneath,
If you want peace
And will have peace.

How fine the skull
It has no eyes,
Nor lips to twist
In bitterness,
Just sockets that see
No starlit skies,
A hollow that can
No wrongs redress.

The skull tells all,
The flesh deceives,
It twists and turns
From lie to lie,
Its form is shaped
By cowardice,
Its texture
By the inward eye.

Search out the skull
Disclose the teeth
Neglect the flesh
Watch not the face
But find the skull
That's underneath.
If you want peace
And will have peace.

Removal of Parts

He had lost confidence in his parts.
They didn't belong
They were not his
They became smaller
Deceitful.

Most especially it applied
To hands and feet, to head
And to those other parts
That had a function
He had never understood.
Mysterious.

Dogs at the door, desperate for out
Their independent life
Infuriated him.
They had no right.
Offensive.

The way they waved
Or turned
Or smiled
Demonstrated.
Even spoke.

The rest of him
Was alright.
It stayed in place
Continued normally.
Behaved.

But those parts!
One day he took a knife

And... cut them off
Starting with the feet
And ending with the head.
Removal of parts.
Satisfactory.

Love's Fancy

Love, infatuation, call it what you will
Blinded me to the fact
Her breath was foul.

Love has such strange, remarkable devices
She can obscure smells
From oral crevices

Rendering most dreadful odours sweet as roses
Heaven sent, whatever
The breath discloses.

Similarly it is with other features,
Bow legs, flat feet, fat arms
And spotty faces.

Love turns all of these idiosyncrasies
Into the most sweet
And bewitching mysteries.

Here though's the rub and mark it well for God's sake,
Should love turn sick
Or maybe fever take

Causing her to die within the lover's heart,
Illusion's tissue will shred
And rip apart.

Hideous the truth will seem, then doubly so,
Ghastly the mouth will reek
And poisonous too.

Arms, legs and teeth so terrible appear
That all the dead in hell
Could cause no fear

To match the lover's now, at her embrace,
　　　Nor cause such pain
　　As sight of her foul face.

The Treacherous Month

Damn you September,
You're a fraud,
Neither autumn nor summer
Yet claiming both.

Pretender!
You have caused more pain
Than all the months and years
Put together,
Again and again.

Deceiver!
Traitor to the heart.
Teller of lies,
Meddler with life's mysteries.
You with your wretched goodbyes.
Get out!

And never bother to return.
From now on
Let August on the 31st
End summer with a blaze,
And autumn come

With October straight away.
No tears, regrets, leave-takings,
Just the steady march on
Into winter,
Heart set, head down,
Hard weather on the way.

Billy

One sees things rather late you know,
And it takes a cat to tell you so.

Pussy, I chased under the bed
With a stick
(A wicked lad was I)
Who later slept on my chest
Purring so weakly,
(He was soon to die)
Wanders in now
Thirty years late,
Wet with rain
And nudges my hand
That held the stick
(A wicked lad was I).

This cat says, "Never mind,
I chase birds too
Like boys chase cats.
You wouldn't do it now
Would you?
Miaow, Miaow!
Cats you see
Are all the same,
One lives on
In another cat,
With another name."

This cat rolls and purrs
The same purr
Of long ago,
And sleeps the same sleep
Through my chest.
The sleep
I used to know.

A Father's Goodbye

If only we could say goodbye now,
Not wait until the end of things.
For if we said it here on the brow
Of night-time, with summer still holding
The hills, there wouldn't be sorrow.

Only fun would possess us two chums;
We would point down the valley and laugh
At the distance, and how the road runs
On and on. "You're never tough enough
For that trek Dad. Wait till morning comes."

"Tougher than you mate," I'd wink at him.
"I'll see you later on, goodbye."
And so saying, I'd stride off into dim
Uncharted country with voice and eye
Untroubled; joyful to the brim.

Depression

There was no cause for the mood
It came on him like a black fly
Out of the untroubled blueness.
He never knew why.

The sun touched his shoulder
But the fly settled down
On his hand for ever.
It was something he could never
Never understand.

Walmer Beach

Intense irritation
Contrasting strangely
With rural peace.

Sudden observation
Of this anomaly
Giving some release.

October in the sky
Reflected on sea
Illuminates his face.

Pierces through eye
And into brain. Mercy
Thus to him
Through nature's grace.

The Art of Creation

Anyone can be a poet.
You just take up a pen,
Write down a few words,
And show it
To family or friend.

And then
There may be
A certain...
How shall I say,
Blankness?

But in due course
Strangled sounds
Will be noted
(By the poet)
Pleasant gargling ones.

This shows approval
And I have found
These happy noises
Can be indefinitely prolonged
By the production
Of further efforts.

The Seasons

Circle

Was it just a heavy dew
Or had it rained?
It was the eve of November
Fifty-third time round
Nor had I lost or gained
Anything since childhood
That I could remember.
Everything remained just
As it was then, stained
By Time, but yet unstained.
Was it only dew
Or had it rained?

November 2001

Winter

We touched, and the wind soughed
Through the open window,

Held hands while clouds
Played horses in the sky.

We lay still, as the moon
Embroidered our stillness,

Slept then a winter sleep,
One body, you and I.

January

Cat on boiler
Dog in basket,

Winter outside
Colder inside,

Dust uneasy
In between the

Sage and thyme
On tidy shelves.

Clothes hung neat
Around the cat.

Breakfast sins
Washed up, away.

A pristine floor
Gleams guilty, clean.

Someone's crying
In the kitchen.

Something's wrong
Inside the kitchen.

Maybe it will
Never leave me.

Monday morning.
January.

A Married Man's First Poem for a Year,
Written at the Age of Forty-six, in a Period of
Personal Decline

So shall we straighten out
This crooked stick of thought
And say that there is not,
Nor has been, neither is to come
Any enlightenment, but only
This one square of pavement,
This corner of the street,
These steps into my home.

A chill wind keeps company
Upon the porch. I pause and turn
Acknowledging the space where
Someone might have been if...

Ah, January without
And January within.
This wind tells all
I need to know.
This greyness is
My brightness now.

January 1995

Stars

It's good that I've been brought down by your leaving,
As far down as possible,
Right to the base of myself.

From this point I can look and see the sky,
Night and day the same, your face is there,
Darkly bright with me.

And those stars, endless,
Endlessly consoling, come close,
Tight inside my chest, and shine.

January 2001

February Fool

Are you surprised that you should feel this way,
This day of all days,
The cruellest in the calendar?

You should know! It cuts pretence quite away,
Erases dreams, shows exactly what you are,
This day.

You cannot hide from its particular light
Which streaks the corners of that prison
In your head.

February the first! February fool! It brings a choice
For fools, this day. A birth? A death?
Each with its special pain.

The Colourist

Grey-coated February
Arrives, sits down
Upon the stones and
Paints the sky.

He colours himself in
With confidence.
He knows his rights,
He follows January.

What is the shade that's
Neither blue nor grey?
He tints the sea with that.

My eyes reach out
To touch this page
With words of spring.

Walmer beach, 15th February 2000

Spirit

Something about your room today,
Not important,
Just different,
A scent of you perhaps, the way…

The sunlight streamed
And was a stream connecting us,
Connecting me to where you were.
Or so it seemed.

I called upstairs,
Asked your sister,
Had she sensed you too then,
A lightness, beyond tears?

"Yes, when the sunlight beamed,"
She said, upon your bed,
You'd come into the room…
Or so it seemed.

Diana

Silver, Gold,
Incarnadine,
Both passionate
And passionless,
Of change, infinite.
Changeless.
Still, over our
Sorrows, rampant
Across desire,
Cold witness to birth or
Love by hill or stream.
Watcher of death in
Ward or room.
Diana
My sentinel be.

26th February 2001

Hope

Hope is February's ground
Softening under sun.
Hope is green,
Is sound,
Light in darkness,
A cry, a life,
Death sometimes
But in itself
Without death.
Hope's a daffodil,
A feather or leaf,
Undetermined
In the wind.

Hope is light over
Rooftops, shining on
Other people's lives,
Their tomorrows,
A tree reflected
On a wall in the
Casualness of sunlight,
A family of croci,
So careless,
Out for the day, their
First and final spring.

Hope is all you have
And all the time you have,
Everywhere, endless, and
Always there for you.
Remember this.
Allow it to be true.

Written to Mary Anne in those days
between winter and spring, February 1999

My Best Friend Who Reaps

No,
I wouldn't mind
If he found me now
In February,
Not at all,
And made friends,
Best friends,
Once and for all.

He who's kind
I've heard, to those
Who watch for spring
In water, stone and wind,
Would gently take my
Hand for guidance,
As the light widens
And thought opens
Impossibly
To its own end.

No,
I wouldn't mind
If he would
Find, touch
(At a street corner
Where February
Constructs a wall,
Whitens the mind)
Me,
And take me then
As his best friend
For ever.
Not mind at all.

The Sculptor

March the sculptor strides the beach a frantic fellow eats
a peach throws a stone furious to the sky rages makes a
storm smiles suddenly a tear wets his eye he laughs weeps
bellows he is full of power carves the stones shovels the
sea grey and strong unstoppable he marches on he fills
the rondure of my eyes with light

he's me.

2001

The Room

Suddenly the door was locked and the key to that room,
The place we used to go,
Know each other now and then,
Was hidden.

Who put it away? I don't know, but the same
Person hid the room as well; all at once
It was missing from the top of the stairs too.
Gone.

Sometimes I meet you on the landing, muttering
About the key. You seem to think
If you find it, you will find the room again.
Wrong.

Our eyes meet in a secret pool of sadness and
Puzzlement, but we both know it's
Too late now, and is
Forbidden.

12th March 2001

Driving On

You'd stopped and you didn't know it.
You just went on driving and driving,
Or thought you did, and
The rain was slashing down,
The wind tearing at the car.
You thought you were still going,
In fact you were stationary.
The engine was dead,
It had stalled – long back.
And I wasn't even there beside you.

Etymology

The new words came slowly.

One. then one by one. then twos and threes. it had to be
that way. he knew. it was a birth. the words were there.

Seeds. they had to grow. sown in thought to reap in
sound. foreigners. refugees. he hated them. they prowled
his brain like wolves. They slipped around his head like
snakes. they felined in his mouth. sprang from his
tongue. he spat them out and ten more came. he spat
and spat and fifty more thickened his throat. he spewed and spewed.

then…

There were thousands. regiments. armies of words.
words he did not know at all. they stared at him and
he became afraid. they had no fear. they soared. they
were the future, were the language that will speak
when love has turned away.

his brain had born them but he didn't understand.
he feared these children, hated them but they were
his.

he'd thought them and they lived.

Spring

She sits in the garden, aged since yesterday,
Suddenly. Dogs do that.

Her minutes and her hours speed past mine.
My hours are her days.

Her white beard and brown eyes
Are infinitely gentle.

May covers her, her favourite coat of sun.
She draws me (poor unsettled beast)

Into her circle of age, her slow,
Swift process of farewell.

Her body understands,
She knows more than I

My failure as an animal and man.
Can she forgive that?

The question dissolves in its own stupidity
And her eyes' incredible softness.

Affection between us deepens. She knows,
I know, our years are measured in each other.

I've counted out my days in many dogs
But she can only put her faith in me.

The Loss of Yellow

The forsythia by my garden wall
Reminds me of something
I had forgotten about
Quite a long while ago.

Just an impression really,
Not an event to be
Deliberately recorded,
But a sense, a feeling,

A love of yellowness.
Yellow, sour green, all
Ringing and shining together
In that very first garden.

These are the precious things, but
Complications blur the memories,
Or chase them deep
Into the labyrinthine mind.

Now yellow seems a different colour
And the children's faces
Shine with a harder light. They
Have forgotten their first garden too.

The End of the Tale

As a preparation, he was taken to the trees on the hilltop, where they whispered with the wind and rain, then laid gently at their edge and left there. He was thus protected by the trees but also able to view the far distance, the delectable valleys and remote, untroubled hills, where they blended their colours mysteriously and delicately into sky. That panorama became for him a stage upon which the myriad events of his life floated past in dispassionate re-enactment. The perfect meeting of sky and land on the horizon suggested his own death, and reassured him. When that moment came, his body remained on the earth from which it sprang, and to which it would return in payment of debt; but that part of him which was spirit stepped freely away, absorbed like mist into the light. His passing was in this way a thing of beauty and fulfilment. A circle completed.

Turning Point

Stop!
Street corner,
Apex of the day,

Meeting myself here
Coming the
Other way.

Decision!
Right or left, or
Simply stay

Watching the
Catnapping streets,
The way

Time hangs in them
Late morning,
Idling her June away.

Walmer Lawn Tennis Club

Summer

How can I act with reason
When azure takes me?
Green and yellow assail
My citadel of self,
Turn me from my home
Into the summer fields?
So am I then not I
Nor where I live, but in the grass
And blue, driven and lost beyond.
My face and eyes are walls
And windows of an empty house
Where curl the summer winds,
Where vacant courtyards reach
Up to an empty sky.

It Was Late June

They met at the railway station.
She'd been eating a bun
In the waiting room.
It was a hot afternoon.
She was visiting a relation.

The train was late (as usual)
Death punctual (as always).
She saw him on the platform
And went out to meet him.
A better destination.

Borders

Where
Roof meets rain,
Where
Hill cuts sky
Which
Melts into idea.
Where
Body touches
Spirit.
Walking, seeking
To find those
Borders,
Touch them,
Go across.

June 2000

Home

He comes to a land that is strange to him
but towards which he has been travelling for a long
time. A valley lies ahead. This place is his destination,
he has no further to go. He feels pleasure and mild
surprise, for although he knew he would come here in
due course, he had not thought to arrive so soon. He
looks ahead to the expanse of field and flower, ancient
wood and turbulent river this resting place contains. He
knows he has to find something precious that once
belonged to him, which waits for him here. What is it?
What is it? His memory, so clear when travelling, has
dimmed curiously at journey's end. A lock of hair?
A picture? A handful of dust? With each question his
recollection recedes like an echo into the mysterious
trees ahead. Forgetfulness steals over him like sunlight
and he sits amid the flowers. He begins to play the idle
games of boyhood. He doesn't know it, but has found
what he had lost so very long ago.

Canterbury

Don't worry on your place and time,
You're woven into history,
Tapestried onto pilgrim streets.

The evening bells unite, fuse past
And present into tone,
Sound explanation of your days.

6.00 p.m., 5th June 2001

The Lady

She left him
When he lost
His watch.
Given in a red
Presentation box
When he was
Twenty-one,
He wore it always,
Kept it
Beyond the reach
Of time,
A sign to him
Of better days,
Good fortune.
Aged fifty-one
He lost it
On the beach,
In June.

The fates stirred promptly
As they must
At such events
To pull the strings
Of time and space.
A shadow slid
Across the sun.

Crash!
Waves and stones
Drumrolled
A warning.
He needed none,

Knowing luck
Had stayed
With that token
Of his younger
Days.

June 1998

The Lost Kids

Looking for them now
Every street I go,
Every corner,
Every shop,
Every shop window.

Finding them somehow
Like a faint echo
Of any laugh
Of any child
In any street I go.

Finding them in toys and clothes
In any shop I go,
Every corner
Of every street,
And every shop window.

Finding them in faces
Faces I don't know,
Faces I meet
In every street,
In every street I go.

Finding them in smiles
Like those I used to know,
They break my mind now
In every shop
And every shop window.

For loneliness falls slowly
Lies deep as mountain snow,

In every corner
Of every street,
And every street I go.

Some July in Ashford, Kent

August the Defendant

Sir, it is to be regretted that your undoubted abilities
Should have been degraded to such purposes as these.
Your arrogance has brought you to this pass; your
Downfall one might say. It could have been supposed
Your ancestry of spring and summer would have led to
Better things. Alas, your thirty-one days have proved this
False. They have been a catalogue of mischance and
Deception. Overweening pride, gross humours, anger,
Insolence, have been your sum. You have brought only
Ruin in your wake and deadening of love. Yes, and
Cooling to love's master, desire, as well. Colours have
Sickened under your gaze and fields withered. Flesh and
Eyes are dull. And hopes, hopes? What were they? You
Must go now; whether there is life beyond your reign we
Do not know, but live we must anyhow. We long for the
Certainty of cold.

Sir, you should be ashamed, you are a disgrace,
And it is obvious you must be taught a lesson.

Send him down. Take him away.
Cover his face.

2001

Adult

Summer will never be the same now.
Where used to be a space in August,
A door swinging in the wind, dust
Aimless, circling, there lies a hollow
In my mind, and in my chest, sorrow.

Afterwards

After, Love, after, we felt our hands
Touching, touching,

And they were wind through trees,
Our hands, in their giving and receiving.

And later Love, later
(Though no time was passing),

They were stones, our hands,
Strong in their holding.

5th August 2001

September Song

Dolphins? Porpoises?
No, they were humans
Plunging and dancing
In the waves of
Some eternal sea.
I saw them, marvelling, for
Time had not arrived there,
Had not found them.

Timeless, they were perfect,
Told the story perfectly
Of boy and girl and
Boy-girl love.
Those things as
They were dreamt to be.

Walmer beach, September 1999

Autumn

O Love we see our very Autumn now,
But in our fall we hold each season's prime.
My youth, manhood and age rest on your brow;
Engraved deep, your womanhood on mine.
My March, your April frosts, swift, foolish May,
Our June's richest laughter we hold in store,
For when our darker season comes; then say
Those words of candlelight once said before.
Then Love you are the window to my days
And I your glass to memory's green hour;
So I in you and you in I find ways
To slip the hand of Time's inquisitor.
Reflection then shall fill our wintertime
And faces. I in yours, and yours in mine.

2001

October

Sea you...
Sunbather you, rolling
Tiger-bellied since March, tempting
Spring to tickle your chest
Flirting with April, a
Blush of blue come May,
Joking with June.

Sea you...
Lazy dog you, lying
Dozy through July, motionless,
Argumentative in August,
Feigning a September death.
Now, October stirs you,
Now you flinch and bare your
Teeth, white with fear.

Sea, your
Master's back eh?
Brutal from the north with
Roughing words and
Whip of wind, to flail your back,
To set you on a roar,
To make you run.

Waiting Room

Hold,
We slip away from
Where we are,
We think we are,
From one another.
Tightly now, love, tightly.
Time takes our hands and leads us
Even as we touch, down
Corridors we do not know
To rooms we have not seen.
Strangers we sit, to
Each and to ourselves.
We dare not look into
The other's eyes
But stare ahead
And wait our turn.

And wait.

Because You Were There

The waves said something to both
They wouldn't have said to one, and
Understanding came between us then
That couldn't, were we alone.

The sea is our beauty, Child,
By it we know each other's mind.
Listen to its voice, my last one,
When Daddy's gone. To remind.

To Mary Anne –
Bournemouth beach, 26th October 2000

Sad

Finally
In despair
I went into
My garden.

Counterpoint

The piece of Bach served its purpose
For the middle-aged couple, who
Otherwise might not have done so,
Enfolded and cuddled through the fugue.

The widow's face, encrusted with
"Musts" and "must-nots", opened
Like a child's hearing its first notes,
While the depressed divorcee tapped,

Tapped, tapped his fingers to the beat.
Everything in the room was normal and
Human again. For a while they regretted
Nothing, nor wished for anything more.

November

Careful!
The road narrows, sharply.
The way you once strode down,
Those easy skies, those plains of chance,
Illusion now.

Gone!
You walk separate. The friends you think
Enjoy your company,
Laugh at your satires, have
Slipped down other tracks,
Their own.

Look!
None follow you, none will.
The merriment you hear,
The lights you see, dance,
Flash, only in your mind.

Beware!
This pathway glooms now, steepens;
Ahead, shadows, silence
And inconsolable regret.
No one to tell you "Peace".

Strengthen!
None have trod these steps before,
They are your very own.
Take them boldly, as you
Climbed to light. You leave here as you
Came, alone.

December

So let us take the greatest pleasure known to us,
Of flesh on flesh and skin on skin, its taste through skin;
Arms intertwined in stillness. Marbled in tranquillity.
So still, so still we lie here now, and in this shard,
This fleck of time will be here still, when stars are
Lost, and space is dust inside a stone.

A to Z and a Bit French

Kissing you I knew the city
In your hand I saw its skies.
Your head was Highgate
Your feet Blackheath, and
Your tummy, Battersea, sorry!
And your back, just where
My fingers strayed upon it
Was Trafalgar Square.
Your heart beat in St James's Park;
I met you on the bridge there
And kissed your lips, and
The swans, a pair of them
Drifted towards spring.

Gin

Again

And there they sat – dumb
Upon his desk. It was in fact the
Beginning of October – numbness
Had been the order of the days and nights
Before; urgency, meaning, discovery gone,
Fled down some corridor of fancy,
Faery lights.

There they sat, the poems, dumb
Upon his desk. The autumn sun
Lay on them like a sword. They had done
Nothing except sit and be absorbed
Into the days.

But now his words beat out
Against the anvil of the night,
His words, this riddled man,
With no distortion, pity, lie. Now
In this thread of loosened time
He picked them up and

Touched the sword,
The shaft of light.

Again.

Sound and Fury

Waking one day
He found the words
Had slipped away,
A way of their own,
Had receded,

Rolled backwards
Like a great wave
To the horizon,
Those words he'd said.

He could see them
Like a tiny crest
Before they crossed
The lip of the sky.

Staring after them
He wondered vaguely
Would they ever
Come again
To trouble him,
Waking one day.

Happiness

Let her happen here in my doorway
Where she left unnoticed
Down the years. Or in this stone
Whose colours hold the sky, this
Canterbury street where blossom
Takes a brief dominion on our eyes; a
Street where sorrow has undone
So many. Let sadness go now,
Drift away in pink and white,
Drifting, as she came, in spring.

Deal Beach

In this sky I dream.
In this water flow my hopes.
They curl and break
Around my feet.
On the sand there
Forms a question.
In this stone I gaze
Into my heart.

Philosophy

A return to the older ways
So give me for my age
Marjoram and thyme
Cicely sweet, parsley, sage
A handful steeped,
Lavender, rosemary,
Garlic, and a crush of
Juniper for memory,
A rhyme of sleep
To round the days.

Primroses

Something's happened by the apple tree.
Back, drunk, March
Or is it late February?

And there they are in the dark
Shining into my darkness
Shining right at me.

Spring has done this.
Primroses have happened,
They have broken the ground,

Have come to me.

13th March 2003

Washing Line

I feel change
But it is only sky
Shifting its place
Above me,
The weather.

The washing is
Almost dry but...
It may rain,
Soon.

I take it in
Hurriedly,
Not seeing
The blossom
At my feet.

To Be Free

…until one day
He made a thing
From no thing

…or one day
Found a thing
From no where.

Like a thrush
It flew into
His hands

Like a bird
It lay there
Was beautiful.

He wondered
At it, held
It tightly.

No one had
Ever held this
Bird before.

It was entirely
His own.
He

Opened both
His hands
And let it fly.

Words

Words become
difficult
strange
dry

a course without water   a room with no door
they
are   *enclosed*
not   *thick*
what   *turbulent*
they   *confused*

say   *deafening*

they   *deadening*
are
not   **They kill**
what   **with noise**

they sound any more

they have become unwords

we have to thin them
out
prune

find light
between the letters
tone
beneath the sound

in the desert wandering we found them moonlit under cliff by
tree fireside

questions formed burned into the future now in the city we lost
them by roadside
pavement or river grey, grey, grey, on telephones and screens they
died

those first words

Education

First there were the questions, later
Came answers. Then there were
Both questions and answers;
We knew them well.

The questions faded and
Only answers remained; so
We forgot the questions and
Their answers had no meaning.

The answers faded also. Now
There is no question and
No answer, no why or because.
Is this the truth?

The Other Place

"And is there," the student asked, "is there…" – he hesitated, struggling for a word – "…another place?" The wise man cocked his head like a robin, full of intelligent enquiry and understanding. The student continued, refreshed by his beneficence: "And is there then a… heaven?…" The word almost collapsed on unused legs: "…a heaven that we find… and go to afterwards?"

The Master answered at once in a surprisingly direct manner as though he'd been expecting such a thing. "Why yes, of course, it's still there," he smiled. "Still there, just." His face grinned like a Persian cat's. "Think of it as a garden, in your mind, or somewhere else, but a garden, very overgrown, very overgrown, unused," he smiled, "unvisited, the gate locked with a rusty chain. Whether you find it or not is chance, pure chance." The master's face was changing now, becoming somehow flattened like a wall. "And if you find it you may never even know and pass it by, and if you do know you may not have the key, have left it behind, forgotten it." He screamed with laughter: "Forgotten the key…" and his laugh was terrible and true, his face stone, with fissures running down its cheeks, a wall, a wall with creepers and tendrils on his brow, and in his eyes there shone the radiance of ancient flowers. Then he was gone, had never been.

And the student forgot the question.

Sound Sense

In the chord there was
Silence.

She found it with surprise
Having long understood that

Sound expressed meaning
Her sense of beauty.

Touching it, almost
By accident

She touched the law
Of opposites

Found the void
We seek

Wonder
Behind the tone.

The Two Gifts

I give you a hundred pounds
Because you are my youngest daughter,
Not because you deserve it particularly
Now, or as I might have done unthinkingly
Once, by reason of your beauty,
Your laughter…

But simply…
Because you are my youngest daughter
And all the best and worst of me
Is like a sea in you, and
Where my poetry, that other gift,
That bird, has flown to rest.

The Bend

Some walks never end
Like this one. Look! As
We follow the bend
Trees wave like seaweed
In the sky and the
Great fist of the wind
Seizes the valley
Trying to find us
And winkle us out
Into our future.

But it won't, we are
Secure here in this
Glade of permanence.
Nothing changes here,
We have been walking
Forever on this spot
Just on the bend
Of the moment…

But the
Road winds uphill and
We come to the edge
Of the trees. Beyond
Wind separate tracks
Of our two lives.

Turning we walk back
Through the woods and talk
Of things we know and
Love, and reach that bend
Again. I won't forget
You here, this place
And in this time
My friend.

An Old Man Waits His Time

Curled up in bed
A sparrow
A seashell

The old man
Waited
Listened

The wind...

The wind
Grew itself
Like a god

Gently

It played
With his
Windows

Wildly

It played
With
His windows

Strangely

It sang
There...
Told him

The truth
Of his fancies
Dreams

He knew
He knew
He knew

Curled up in bed
A leaf
A seashell
A sparrow
He listened

Waited

For the wind.

Change

Strutting on hopefully
               hopelessly
In the rain, something
Lost there, something
Found here
Neither of them known
                 Properly
Neither of them
Bound to occur
           to be,
Remnant of past ruin
Shred of the future
Rag and bobtail bits of
                      time,
                      flotsam.
This is what it is to be
                    human,
Lost
Found
Against the wall,
On the street,
In the rain.

This is what it means
               to be
Trapped endlessly,
               ultimately
               ultimately
Free?

Things to Do

First, a list
To conceal the page,
My brother, phone him
Then the bank
To rearrange
That wasted
Bit of future,
That meeting
Of no minds.
Now… rewrite
Next Sunday's
Hours…
Collect today
Up in your arms
In disarray, half
Dropping it,
Its papers, keys,
Place them near the door
Quickly now…
Fumbling
Another call, and another?
Maybe not
And then… what then?
That other thing
Never listed, never said.

To find and wake
The king within
Who will not rise
Who cannot rule.

Notice

No!

I can't do it any more.
Sorry, I've
Suddenly realized
Unexpectedly
Without warning
And have to get out
At this very station

Now.

A quiet place
Unfrequented,
Verdant,
Overgrown, no
Ticket barrier
I see. Almost
My very own.

Wander as a child
Into the fields
Beyond.

Reading *The Leopard* by Giuseppe Tomasi di Lampedusa marked
a turning point and place of reassessment. One realized, in
tandem with that book, that a man in his mid-fifties must see a
falling away of the fields below him, an opening of the skies, and
a clear, untroubled point on the horizon.

The Reason Most People Have Traffic Accidents Is...

That they see their road behind
Spread out in front of them
But not the road ahead.

That face in Chelsea on the
Embankment, those lips curved
Cruelly by the moon,

Those words dragged out
Reluctantly, meaning nothing
Absolutely nothing at all.

A smile of contempt was it?
Was it? Or lust? Bitter nothings
Beneath a chocolate sky?

Coldly, under strip-lighting,
A judgement made which
Never could be then unsaid.

Those are the reasons
Why most people
Have traffic accidents,

When the road behind
Meets the road ahead.

Children's Addresses

3 Essex Court – the downs behind
4 Wolverton Road – God knows!
Ladlands Estate, badlands those.
Overhill Road – the eye of London town,
27 Whitefield Close,
Just round the corner but
As far as Africa to us.

Those names, those resonances,
Those sounds, those places which are homes
For kids who grew there, but never
Homes for those who came,
For them only places on a road
Between the first home and something else,
Addresses whose three words hold
Whole histories of days and nights
Of questions why, why we came
And why we left, and what it was
We left behind; in those first homes.

Shrine

There was light on the stone
And something between the stone
And light, shone.

There was the sound of a piano
Then something like gold between
Ear and tone.

There was the touch of our fingers
And something we could not hold slipped
Between them

And I wondered and wondered
What was its name.

The Huntress

The wind will claim you in the end.
Listen!
Outside the window, she prowls round your domain.
Yes?
She sighs and groans, she's longing for you.
Take heed
Of what I say, she'll have you in due time,
She'll wait.
Hark! Her voice contains the spirits of all men,
Her prey.
You hadn't thought of her like that before
Had you?
All your hopes, your fantasies, beliefs,
Beliefs!
Just dust beneath her wings.

Rain

The rain reminisces of you.
Its drops are the tears you shed
On our doorstep when you
Flung your arms around me.
Your boyfriend had been untrue.

And now and now? Well
That's the point of rain isn't it? It
Washes me through and through, and
You and your boyfriend are memories,
But the rain remembers you.

The First Day of Spring

The two old shitters came out to play
One an old fart of a jag, 1970s, he
An old fart of a banker, 1980s. Gay
Seemed the season and it seemed to say
A sort of well done to both of them
For sort of making it. They
Smiled at each other, rusty, dented, grey,
Blinking suspiciously in the daylight,
They'd been each other's pride and joy,
Wife, father and mother, and now?
Just a couple of old shitters out, but hey!
Still blinded by love.

Gay seemed the season
Brightly shone the day.

Queer

The old ladies at the bus stop were dead.
They didn't know it of course
And would have said
Had it been mentioned,
"What nonsense that young man talks."
But it was true
And I knew
But didn't say,
Just read their faces,
Wrote this down instead.

Omens

There had been signs from that other place,
Aye,
A picture falling in a quiet room at night
And,
More worryingly, a phrase of
Birds
Unfolding skywards from a winter tree,
Yes,
That held its arms wide after their
Flight
Piteously it seemed, longingly.
And
Then the sun, that harbinger of
Doom
Strode down the fields of memory
Trailing
Blood upon the hills, a stain…
This
Last and those before gave warning of a path
To come.

The Solution

Touch is the answer to your
Question, why.
I touch you,
This is my reply.

There is no movement
On these cruel lands
But finds its peace
Beneath our hands.

Hold it my love, the answer,
Under this bitter sky.
My hand will
Take your question,
Give reply.

Bird Strike

A message went across the lands, the seas,
Stop!

Across the kingdoms, the democracies,
Dictatorships, the cruel and the kind,

The Pope's house, the Sultan's home,
The believers and the unbelievers.

Stop, stop, stop now, do not sing again.

A ripple of wings, a tsunami of bird-thought
Circled swifter than death's kiss this globe
Of ours

And the dawns went silent and
There were those who lay in half sleep

Who wondered at this new sound of silence,
Turned into their troubles, slept again

And there were those who had lost their souls
Who heard neither sound nor silence

And slept, and slept.

But anyway

This marked the ending of our time.

To W.W.

This Be the Month

November tells no lies,
Nor takes them. Even
The twelfth month, her sister,
Deceives a spring, but
This goddess sees you
As you are, vacant,
Open to the clouds,
Bare-branched,
Defiant, in
Solitude…

In prayer?
Who knows
Who cares?
Not November.
With pitiless hand
She measures you,
With her amber pencil
Draws you into her scape
Of land, towns, streets,
Her skies. November.

Steps

I am concerned with
Coming out of doorways

Into sunlight and
Finding things

Not quite as they
Were before.

The feet move forward
Into the courtyard

But the steps go back
Into the rose garden

Into childhood
And that other light

That will be
Could be now,
And was,
Once before.

Heart

Inside me is one who walks
Winter and summer
Day and night
Always the same
He walks.

Inside me is one who walks.
I listen to him now
Against the pillow
One two, one two
Always the same,
He walks.

Inside me is one who walks.
Let's see his face now
This stranger
Yet friend too
Who walks inside
Always the same,
Who walks.

Inside me is one who walks.
Is his face happy
Or sad? No,
Neither of these.
A mask, it sees
Only ahead to
An absolutely
Predetermined spot
On the horizon
Where he will stop, dead,
This one who walks inside,
Always the same
Who walks
And walks.

Inside me is one who walks.
A long journey behind,
Rivers, forests, seas.
The road winds uphill now,
Ahead? Rain, wind, snow?
I don't know, I know only
His tread against the night
Against my pillow
Always the same
Always the same
He walks
And walks
And walks.

December

And in that month
There came a spring
Suddenly, and so a
Makeshift group of birds
Gathered themselves
Together and
Surrounded me
As in a choir,
A ragged lot,
And sang to me,
And I was filled with
Mystery of the time,
And wonder at every thing,
In that December.

23rd December 2002

January

This January spooks me. It's
Not like others I have known.
A death seems imminent
Perhaps a birth.
The wind is full of rumours
On my window panes.
They shake with news.
Nothing seems as it is.
From uncertainty grows light.
To live beyond the moment
I must change.

January 2002

February

...is long
Her beginning
Is not known
Her ending lost
In memory.
February, Ah!
Drink her water
Read her skies.

February 2002

Daffs

I sniffed you almost…
Suspiciously.
What were you doing?
Why were you there?
It seemed…

Hardly fair
That you should be
So radiantly young, so
Ignorant of age,
So beautiful.

I, a temporal creature
Sniffed you, yes
Almost suspiciously,
Rather like an animal,
Puzzled by the eternal
On my sideboard there.

February 2002

Change

As you age seek the hills.
Find your peace
And there...

Shed vanity of years,
Cast it with your shirt
Upon the ground.

Make spaces in your
Thoughts as spaces are
Between these clouds.

Be taken
And be taken
By the wind.

The Pilgrim's Way, above Godmersham Park

Solstice

All is poised, the
Summer in our fingers
Above our heads,
Winter below us, southern
Beneath our feet;
Autumn to the left
Spring on our right hand.
Everything moves,
But now,
All is poised.

Horses

Walk, climb, stand, stare,
Breathe, sweat, be…
Be like the horses, human,
In this bare field,
No thought of
You and I.

Be no man, yield
Yourself unhuman
To the clouds
And wind, to
Grass and trees,
The healing sky.

The Pilgrim's Way, above Godmersham Park.

Downs Road, Walmer

Do not go up that road
Nor even look its
Lazy length to where
A school sits on the hill.

Turn, turn away now
Lest its azure space
Remind; children's laughter
Lead you down a longer path.

No, fold your papers
Fumble with your keys,
Safely to the shops now.
Stay in forgetfulness.

Waiting Room 17.56

Where are you?
In a waiting room.

How do you know?
It says so,
The sign.

What time is it?
4 to 6.

How do you know?
The clock,
Tick tock.

Why are you here?
To catch a train.

Where are you going?
Out.

Why?
Because someone asked me.

But really why?
—

But really why?
I don't know.

What are you really doing?
I don't know.

What are you then?
I don't know
Either.

Where are you really going?
Nowhere.

Where have you come from?
Nowhere.

What will happen?
Nothing.

What will really happen?
Nothing,
Once more nothing.

Journeys

Provide an answer
If not a solution.
Journeys
By car or train
Between living space
And destination,
They contain
Neither the furies
Nor the half-life
That those houses hold.

Journeys!
Call them…
Truces, time warps,
Interludes… where
Jealousy nods off, where
Anger smiles and chats,
Look! Failure staring blankly
Out at passing cows.

Journeys,
Where letters on the mat
Open no trembling hand,
No mirror in the hall
Gives notice of your fate,
Stares at a face of fear.

Metamorphosis

The man who had forgotten

How to smile stood
On his step, became
His step, peered out
Across the street,
Became his street,
His face the pavement
Grey.

Alignment happened,
Of his face with wall,
With hedge, with sky.
His shade turned brown,
Green-brown, grey-blue,
Blue-grey. His mouth

Became the cat's
Still as a whisker
On a wall
At night's edge.
His cat's eyes
Locked the past,
Prevented it from
Coming in or
Going out.

His hands which linked
The ground and sky
Forbade the watch to tick,
A future to occur.

The Use of Memory

…and that which was lost
May yet be found.

What I told you once
In November when
The dog-eared wind
Raced round the first house
Tore up the first garden

Rattled the skies
The nervous
Fruit-gum skies
Chased the cat
Up the tree
The first cat
Shook it down
Again

Again
Remember?

You may
You can
You will
You must
Remember
When…

Find it true
Truer even, what
I told you once
Then

In your own
November.

Streets

Streets of the future blaze before me,
Dazzling, strip-lit. And there I am
Confused, huddled, purblind
By windows, rain beating
On that parched forehead...

Streets not taken, streets that
Never should have been taken,
Frantic, scurrying, running
Ahead, running behind,
Streets of age that turn
Mysteriously, brokenly
Lamenting a decision,
Those decisions, that came

Only because of fear.

Now, on this corner I wait.
Now! What now? What now?
But now is already gone,
Is yet to come, is never,
Now is all I have left,
And now is narrowing
Slowly, rapidly, stupidly
To some point
Of no decision,
No return.

I look ahead.
Those lights are false,
They fade into opacity.
I turn around and see
The past that never really was.

That also I reject.
Its thick-textured confusion
No more explains or justifies
Anything.

At all.

I turn three times
And face myself
At last, in the eddy
Of the minute.

All must
Tend towards
Simplicity,
Can ebb into
The present time,
The now that
Is my own.

If I so choose.

Behind

The back yard's
My problem
I can see that now.

Other worlds can wait
But anyhow they're
All contained herein.
Bricks, paint pots, leaves,
Other things, other things. How
Will I ever get it clear
And live easily, freely,
Untroubled by the
Detritus of days.

The vulpine wind lopes
By my hunting ground
And sniffs unease,
A prey. Houses,
Rooftops, towns
Peer down on me. Skies
Question if I live yet,
Scan my time.

Dust must be piled on dust
And leaf on leaf,
Memory on memory
On faint regret
(The things one
Didn't say)
And swept
And stocked
And binned

In my back yard.

?

After much travel
He came to a place
Where everything was hard,
The sky, the ground,
Iron both, clanging
Off each other.
To walk was hard
To breathe, to see
Was hard.
To love
And hate
Also
Hard.

But all these things
He did, as men must
Who tread an iron
Ground beneath
A surging sky,
Bitter cliffs around.

He asked of those he saw
Beside him why this was.
Some said the past,
Some said the future
Catching up with them,

And some said it was
Just this stony patch
Of ground. But then he saw
That those he asked
Were shadows of himself
Reflected on the stars,
Shadows that cloaked him
All alone around.

Onwards
Onwards
Daywards
Nightwards
Forwards
Backwards
Encircling
Himself
He went
Across this
Iron patch of ground.

Home Town – Deal

The bank is red – red brick.
To the side, a precinct,
One of those intended
For community.
Ahead – a high street where
A thousand times
Your steps have taken you,
A thousand days
Have watched you pass,
A thousand hopes
Lit lamps.

Winter afternoons.

Enlightenment comes casually
In Sainsbury's, weakly,
Down aisles, by checkout tills,
Counting the cost of years,
Watching dumb beauty
Tap, tap away her days,
Autumn scuttles past the cars
Outside, his coat turned up,
Hat pulled down,
Ragged, unnoticed.
Old man you are.
Old.

To the side, a precinct, yes,
Down there – a sandwich bar.
November is too chill for this,
Chewing, watching, beast-like
The half-life of the town –
Your town, your streets, your days,

Your friends? who know
Not you, but someone else
They think they see?
Hello! Hello!
Friends who are unable
To be friends.

Human are you? No! Inhuman? No!
A god, a joke? Maybe, yes,
Something of the four.
This place is ground
Beneath your feet,
Inside your bones,
A common ground,
Your ground to love.
Cold you are,
Benumbed you are,
Alone.
You
Are
This
Town.

Deal High Street

The pan pipes played by the Peruvian refugee
(Alpa Kalpa – Andean music) had stopped.
Or rather he'd given up playing them,
His music hushed by the North Sea mist.
Caesar found the same in Deal.
"Isn't it nice?" the girl who served
The sandwich said. "So peaceful."
Yes, it had been nice, but only because
Of a faint nostalgia for other lands.
It didn't belong here but nothing does. An
Unaccustomed silence queened it awkwardly,
Time rippled through the High Street,
Faces warped like beasts or gods.
Celts?

People hurried on edgily as people on
The edge of things will do. The edge of the world.
Unsettled Englishers, more refugeless
Than any refugee, anyone upon your streets,
Faces pulled westwards, towards beyond,
Towards the hills, to Avalon.
Unseeing eyes yearning the temple cliffs,
The final sea.

November 2003

In Memory of... Who Enjoyed This View

I am become a benchman now.
I used to pass unglancing
Or with disdain those warriors
Whose faces are a mirror of the sky
Whose eyes reflect the universe
(Look closely and you'll see the stars).
Purposefully striding nowhere
I used to think – have they nothing
Better to do than sit, is that their life?
Thermoses, sandwiches?

I did not see beneath their pallor
Their drab coats and sweaters
The radiance of October burn
The passion for the sea
The yearning for the south,
So deep, so far, so near.
Nor could
I see.

But now
I am become a benchman too.
Look through my eyes and
You will see the stars.

Walmer beach

Spirit

The sloe gin
Was bottomless, or
So it seemed to them,
Husband and wife,
As they gazed
At the sea of it,
The ships of it,
In the glass flagon
On their sideboard,

The ships of it
Sailing.

Purple, mauve,
Green sometimes,
Sometimes red,
Opaque.

The juice of it
Ah!
The juice of it,
Tasting,
Tasting.

Again the sky,
Again its birds
Soaring.

It gleamed
At them in their
Elderly confusion,
Providing both
A remedy and
Staid solution
To the ills of age.

Blended in autumn
The drink became
A distillation
Of their days,
Sipped in memory,
Taken in communion.

Photography

I didn't realize
You were saying goodbye
In that photo.
No more did you, a teenager
Waving on a Welsh road,
Waving a long, slow farewell
Down the years – a farewell
As it should be said
Between wayfarers, between
Father and daughter...
A smile, a friendly hand,
The crest of a hill.

The camera looked past you
Dispassionately
And told the future.
There was a spray of mist
I remember
And then beyond, a forest
Which has no end.

Fortuna

Out of all those mornings
All those nights
Which were part of years
But longer in themselves
Than years...
Something has come
Something unexpected.
Out of greyness, cold,
Impossibility, the days
Whose only hope was night,
The nights which watched
The days to come...
From something unspeakable,
A struggle that saw no light,
From darkness, yes darkness,
Has grown a flower.

I love you.

Tonic

The Poet Utters

The poet coughed.
It was true he had nothing to say
But felt somehow he ought to say it.
He coughed again, and his face
Assumed the questioning look of
One of those Japanese mushrooms
One sees in better Sainsbury's.
His mouth formed a perfect replica
Of a chicken's arsehole.
"If," he said, "If only," and looked
Towards the window sadly.
It was raining. It was enough.
Everyone was moved and
Somehow he had said it all.

Mirror, Mirror

In the room
Where she died
He paused.
He sat down
Scratched his head
Fiddled with his hands.
He wondered why
He had come here.
There had been
A question, but
What it was…

In the mirror
A tap dripped.
A mirror contains time
Until it is broken.
One should never,
Never break mirrors.
Then you break the past.

It was the first of February
He remembered.
He smiled.
He felt change

Upon him.

Attic

Close the skylight, best
To let it settle now
This dust

To filter through
Silently
This light.

These walls
Are my abode,
My sanctuary

Against without.
Inside, we must refer
To history for sense

To beams and motes
And echoes found
And lost.

First Day of School

Why rush the folding of a sheet?
Outside, the school bus stops,
And faces, questions forming
Which will find no answer
In a class, peer through
My window, deeper than a sea,
At one who cannot tell them now.

I smile and frown. Why rush
The folding of a sheet?

The Farm

What will become here
We cannot say.
This house, locked
In a loop of stream
Between yesterday
And tomorrow, seems
To have no past or
Destination we can
Glean from fading
Light.

The black hills lower
Discontentedly
Ahead, denying
A next valley, and
Behind, our river
Leaks into the mist,
Reminding us of
Something slipped away,
Something never quite
Right.

We cannot say, we
Cannot say or dare
To think of where
We are, or why we
Ever came, or where
We might take
Flight.

A Retired General Plays
The Pathétique Sonata

Beethoven is marched along the keys.
The General… plays his fingers
Like Wellington's stragglers
By God they frighten me
Across the whitened fields of time.
A drum begins to beat in iron brain.
Glinting with flash of steel
His soldier's eyes see crotchets,
Quavers, minims, semibreves.
His nose drips like the drip of rain
Slow, from a tent's edge at dawn, he
Has seen everything, sordor, despair.
Damn! A false note, a soldier falls,
Shots echo across a running field,
A chord is born.

Big Brother

The Poo Police are watching you
Beware of what you do
They watch your hands they watch your bags
And where you place the poo.

And if indeed you pick it up
Or stand there skulkingly
Pretending you see a pleasant view
Across the briny sea.

Alack! Unhappy modern man
For you no longer blue
The lissome sky or greengage sea
Your eyes are glued in poo.

Alack! Depleted Englishman
Who fought at Waterloo,
You wouldn't do much good there now
Too busy scooping poo.

But we are all policemen now
And watch the doggies poo
See if our neighbour picks it up
Or just admires the view.

The Poo Police are watching us
Beware of what we do.
Their eyes a-glint with dread intent
Watch where we pop the poo.

Spaces

Clouds

Her thoughts, as white clouds in a summer sky, simply would not
be hurried on.
Sometimes they seemed to stand still, at others they mysteriously
shifted their place and merged, emerged and reconvened. It was
curious just lying there and watching them pass or not, beginning
to wonder how long a moment will endure...

View from the Bed

Each slate became a word.
She stared in disbelief,
Her words had formed a roof
Which covered all the sky.

Street

Geography is being there.
History is holding hands
In this street, now. Listen,
There is a fountain across
The road. Can you hear it?
Memory may follow after this.

Fresno, California, Christmas Eve 2006

Response to Paul Patterson's Clarinet Concerto, 2nd Movement

We have deeps here, yes, in this cavern, opening

into sky, water?

Sky also can be deep, we
can travel downwards into sky.

We have song here, yes,
but what is the singer singing about?…
We know but we don't know
In some ways we don't want to know
It would be better not to know
maybe.

Why unbuild a palace made of peace?

A cough at bar thirty-three did not interrupt but belonged
to this.

The thing about this music is that
it allows. Look

it takes you by the shoulders
and says stop, just stop for once.

A double bass arrests
reminds us of mortality.

So he's a bird this chap
a slow and ancient bird.
He flaps heavily
absorbedly above
dominions.

At the end a vast crescendo as he lands and his wings flutter into pianissimo after flight. It rains then. Or is it just after the rain, and we hear only the last drops falling on the sea?

He sings a final tune. "Tell me why is the sky so blue?"

But this is your cavern also.
Why don't you write upon the wall?
You will leave no other memory.

The Path

In dreams you came to me then,
You were smiling, there had been rain.

There was a garden we had walked through,
Often in laughter, sometimes in pain.

It seemed I spoke to you then, but
My lips moved soundless, in vain.

Many years, many, had passed then.
You would not return again.

Upwards

Roofs are good
Because they climb.

You want to join them?
It can be done.

I knew a man
Who stared and stared

At a romance of sky
Until one day

The cut of spring
Upon him, he rose,

Unfolded hidden wings
And flew away.

Roof

These roofs   have much   to answer for

Arrogant   strutting their stuff   across

The fields   arguing the toss   with clouds

They tell more   of those   they shelter

Than   the guarded   know

Red   vain   brutish

Bastards

They foretell

Their

Fate

Passage

Give me a corner of March
A street, a wall,
Something to lean against, clouds,
Yet a sharp fall

Of rain against my face. And
That's about all
I want now to reaffirm
My place and the call

Of spring in this withering
Of my timefall,
Sharp in the last few years.
But not quite all,

A corridor of sky, yes,
So fiercely tall
Giving no reasons, answers.
Yes! That is all.

Tide Out

The sea had retreated
Gone out.
People still came to the beach
Looked about
As if it were yet there.
It was not.
They sensed something was wrong
But what
They couldn't say.

It was the same with him
Gone away.
People still came to see him
Each day,
As if he was still there
At play.
They sensed something was wrong
But what
They couldn't say.

Gone out,
Retreated,
Wrong.
Gone away.

The Turn

He dreamt of wolves then
Which signified the turn.
Wolves mean change
In the dreambook.
A journey had begun.

There were hundreds of them
Gathered there
With their keepers.
It was very dark.
There was no sun.

There was a long hill and
A stone wall I remember.
A few muttered words
That was all.
We began to run.

Letting Go

It wasn't as if it mattered, as
He placed his hands on the table
As he stood in the garden
The sky around his feet.
Or facing the kitchen wall
Hands lost among forests
And hills. It wasn't as if
It mattered at all.

Or walking along home paths
Made sudden by spring,
Touching pen to paper
Trying a word or two,
Another, then another,
Letting it rest, March
A soft wound inside his heart.
It wasn't as if it mattered, after all.

The Painter

It was just the feel of the brush,
Not that he could paint or draw,
He was too old for that, just
The feel of it in his hand,
A possibility. Only this.
Like the sky opening
In some strange way,
Night into morning,
Into remote colour
After a storm.

Just the feel of it
Gave him delight.
Holding the brush
He drew a line.

The Gates

The gates crash down
Our eyes meet
Through the bars
The tips of fingers
Touch through steel walls.

On either side
The azure light
Of freedom shines.

The gates crash down, Ah!
How our hands are riven
Now just our smiles
Meet through steel
In empty halls.

Behind, before
The azure
Freedom shines.

The gates crash down
Now also dark divides
The space between us.
Are you there?
Am I your friend
After all?

The gates crash down.
Outside the azure
Freedom shines.
And falls.

Fold

The truth lies in the hands the truth sits in the hands the truth
is not in face or eyes or voice the   truth folds into hands not
shoulders nor the forward step nor backward look but sleep or
wake or night   or   day   the   truth
is   in   the   hands
yes

Hold them out Close them tight Move one to left
Move one to right Fold them unfold

They cannot lie these hands   by day or night   although they try

Look at your hands

6th January 2008

Unexpected

...and the steps?
                    Yes
Were January steps
And the stone I walked
January stone

And the hands in pockets?
                         Yes
They were January hands
The mind fresh
And alone

And the unknown street?
                        Yes
A well-trodden one
By me and others
Long gone

And myself?
            Yes
A January man
My step unexpected
And delightful,
Strong.

                    Canterbury High Street, 2008

River

Dreaming of a river then
I found my freedom
And entering softly
As to a silken bed
I swam and the river
Took me and bore
My cares from me.
Silently they
Flowed away.

And swimming on
There was a bridge
Across the stream
Where rapid water ran
And yet another bay.
And I wept then and
Cried, "Oh river, river"
For flowing there was
All men's mystery.
Each man his way.

February 2008

Petrol Pump

No one will smile here
No meeting of the eye
No touch of human hand
On human arm. Only
The click of petrol cap
The clunk of nozzle in
Socket, the tap on
"Pay at kiosk" or "Pay at
Pump". The whispered
Sigh of petrol running in
And running out.

Desolate, desolate man
Who has arrived at this,
A petrol station
On a motorway
In mid-November
In the pouring rain.
Scarcely do much worse!

One has to smile at
Such a failure of
Intent. For you no
Far horizon in
The west or anywhere
But just the metalled road
Before, behind, and
Hands on wheel, a sense of
Having missed the point.

Spring 2008

Moondream

Why the garden is as it is
And why that chair, moonbathing,
Empty of its purpose as a chair
But full of something else,
I will not understand.

And why that dog stares
Blankly at a shaft of shadow
Thinks it is the shade it sees,
And why that door hangs
Loosely on itself
Waiting for the wind
To make it be a door
That bangs and bangs
An answer. Why? Why?

The word rhymes with itself
And understands itself
And watches as I
Stand and stare at this
Become a pattern in the stars.
Dissolve into the dream.

Spring 2008

Later Years

One step forward.
Two steps back.
As I move towards you.
I fall back but.
Our friendship is on track.

Two steps forward.
Four steps back.
As I try to hold you.
It's you I lack.
Our friendship is on track.

Ten steps forward.
Twenty back.
As I reach out for you.
The sky turns black but.
Our friendship is on track.

A thousand steps forward.
Unnumbered paces back.
Oceans of time between us.
But as I try to hold you.
I fall back and back and back.
Our friendship is on track.

February 2008

Two Daughters

Dalziel

Daughter of wheat
Daughter of corn
Daughter of earth
Child of my eye
The mother you are
Of all men, the wife
For whom all men cry

Daughter of the sky.

Child you are of
My fragile seed
Stronger seed than I
You are the salt
The season and
A need answered
First-born one

A reason why.

Lizzie

Daughter of hands and faces
Beaches and skies, who touches
And replaces real things with
Mysteries caught by your eyes.

The moon on water, icy water
Oh draw it for me daughter
That I may know your mind.
For I have seen your kind

Eyes follow me and turn away
Daughter of mystery. I touch
Your hand across the years.
Our fingers trace a child's sky.

February 2008

And One Wife

Nicolette

Nothing can go wrong
If it's OK with you and me.
That's the point of this story
You see.

Tales may come and tales may go
But it's your lips I know only.
For me, there's no other
History.

February's cold may take me
Age falters in spring you see.
But the point of the story
Is always, for me.

14th February 2008

Landscape

When I grow old I
Shall live by a park.

Dark clouds shall gather
There and pass and white

Ones sometimes will
Stand and stare from their

Palaces of light
And under them by

Day children will shout
And mums call like white

Seagulls to their bright
Ones and then by night

Drunkards will lurch by
And stagger on the

Football ground shouting
Follies to the sky.

And I? And I? I
Shall listen quietly

From my chair or bed
And ever so bright

In my being there
And having a park

To keep company
Throughout the days
Throughout the night.

26th March 2008

Back to the Drawing Board

OK, if I was God
This is what I'd do
First pluck out the traffic signs
Then the motorways too.

I'd have a good old Godly fit
Like Jehovah of old
Rend asunder the bank vaults
Melt down and reclaim the gold.

I'd blow up all the factories
The churches and the towers
Replacing them swiftly
With birdsong, trees and flowers.

And lastly I'd eradicate
A virus I called man.
Daft experiment.
Make another plan.

Synthesis

The edge but edge of what?

It lay there waiting for him.

When he came and stood
Above it looking down, they
Recognized each other,
Him and the edge.

Could be of this, could be
Of that, edge of the table
Of the chair, the roof and
Of the sky, the teapot and
The sea. He had become

A border to these things.
He knew he must diffuse
Into their larger whole
To find his peace.

June 2008

Four Moments, Walmer, Kent

1
The caw
Of the
Crow

Told him
To be
Simple.

Dawn.
A thin
Cut in
The mind.

2
The dream
Brought
Peace

It had
Risen
Slowly from

Nowhere
To
Nowhere

And was
Swiftly
Gone.

3
This
Poem was
The best

The first
Brought
Words only

The second
Flew from
A dream

The third
Gave
Rest.

4
Four things
Will
Remain

Night
A kiss
Dawn
Pain

26th July 2008

Walkout

Production in the poetry factory had
Ground to a halt. The workers on
Iambics had walked out, and those
Applying nuts and bolts to the
Quatrains were having a cup of tea.

The assembly lines of octet and sestet
Were smoking fags in the back yard,
Pissed off, and quality control at
Factory gate hadn't bothered to
Come to work at all, at all.

There was an air of lassitude and
Hopelessness plus, the share price had
Plunged. A directors' meeting was
Scheduled that afternoon and earlier
A new apprentice had arrived. His

Name was William
Nicknamed Will.

September 2008